LET GO
OF HOLDING ON TO
THE FAMILIAR AND
COMFORTABLE;
OPEN YOURSELF
TO GROWTH AND
POSSIBILITY.

ALSO BY MEERA LEE PATEL

How It Feels to Find Yourself: Navigating Life's Changes with Purpose, Clarity, and Heart

My Friend Fear: Finding Magic in the Unknown

JOURNALS

Go Your Own Way: A Journal for Building Self-Confidence

Create Your Own Calm: A Journal for Quieting Anxiety

Made Out of Stars: A Journal for Self-Realization

Start Where You Are: A Journal for Self-Exploration

Meera Lee Patel

Bestselling author of START WHERE YOU ARE

learn to let go

A JOURNAL FOR NEW BEGINNINGS

Tarcher

Tarcher

an imprint of Penguin Random House LLC
1745 Broadway, New York, NY 10019
penguinrandomhouse.com

Most Tarcher books are available at special quantity
discounts for bulk purchase for sales promotions, premiums,
fund-raising, and educational needs. Special books or book excerpts
also can be created to fit specific needs. For details, write:
SpecialMarkets@penguinrandomhouse.com.

Book design by Meera Lee Patel and Shannon Nicole Plunkett

ISBN: 9780593717035

Printed in China
10 9 8 7 6 5 4 3 2 1

The authorized representative in the EU for product safety and compliance
is Penguin Random House Ireland, Morrison Chambers, 32 Nassau Street,
Dublin D02 YH68, Ireland, https://eu-contact.penguin.ie.

To you:
for letting go of what was
and inviting what can be

Introduction

When my daughter was a few months old, I took her for a long walk around our neighborhood. She didn't like being strapped in the stroller, but I needed to leave the house: being cooped up all day for months on end had me feeling overstimulated and lethargic all at once. I felt rattled. I needed to get out.

So: In she went, bundled up, kicking and screaming. I tried not to let the cries elevate my blood pressure. I tried to drown them out to the white noise of the birds, the wind, the cars whizzing by. When we reached the crosswalk, I pushed the Walk button and waited. This particular intersection is extremely busy—traffic is heavy, the drivers are aggressive, and I'd seen multiple crashes take place over my few years living in this city.

The traffic light flickered from green to yellow to red. The cars waiting to make left turns made their left turns, but when it was our turn to cross the street, we couldn't. The crosswalk was completely blocked by an oversized pickup truck that had been forced to stop, while trying his best to run through the red light. The nose of the truck was only a few inches from where we stood.

I maneuvered the jogging stroller, with difficulty, over the tall curb and into the middle of the road. Visibly frustrated, I pushed it around a large gray pickup truck. My body had been holding on to stress for months now, and in this moment, I allowed it to course through me: the stress of childbirth, months with little to no sleep, the cortisol spikes from continuous crying, of feeling like everything within my reach was too much and never enough.

The driver of the pickup truck, a man in his midforties, rolled down his window to express his own frustration upon seeing mine. *I didn't see you there,* he yelled at me. *It doesn't matter,* I shot back. *Cars don't belong in the crosswalk.*

Don't talk to me that way, he yelled at my back, while I pushed my crying child across the street. The end-of-May St. Louis sun was like a cool breeze compared to the heat building inside me. I fumed.

I called my sister to vent. I practically screamed the exchange I'd had with the driver at her, noting his irresponsibility and disrespect. He was in the wrong but had the audacity to yell at me? I fumed. We moved on to other topics, but ten minutes later, I found my anger hadn't run out. My blood still felt hot. I still wanted to vent. *Wasn't it ridiculous how that man yelled at me after nearly running me over?*

Yes, she agreed. *I'd feel angry, too. But the moment has passed. Now it's time to let it go.*

* * *

Holding on to certain things, like reasonable expectations, boundaries, and your core values is necessary. These are inner guideposts for forming healthy relationships and setting goals that encourage growth. Conflict arises when we project our expectations of ourselves onto others—and when we hold on to harmful feelings, relationships, and dynamics far past their expiration dates. Learning to recognize when a person or a situation is no longer healthy for you, even if they once used to be, is a necessary skill for navigating life with an open heart and mind.

A few of the key practices that guide this journal are:

1. A belief in your own infinity. The resources that you have to offer yourself and others—compassion, love, knowledge, friendship, courage—aren't finite. You will not lose them if you share them with another person, even if that relationship eventually falters or breaks.

2. The power of forgiveness. Holding on to resentment leads to emotional defeat and nurtures an inability to move past painful experiences. Forgiving another person, or yourself, is not a sign of weakness; rather, it is an indication of courage and strength.

3. **The importance of reflecting and changing course.** Every person is forced to recalibrate the version of the life they thought they'd have with the one they are living. Those who can learn from their experiences, examine and re-align their values when necessary, and look ahead rather than behind—are far more equipped to cultivate a strong sense of self. These people build the self-confidence necessary for taking risks and remaining vulnerable, even when facing loss and grief.

4. **The power of letting go.** An open heart will remind you of who you are and where you want to go. Letting go is a practice in maintaining your own health. By cleansing yourself of what no longer serves you, you ensure your heart can remain open.

* * *

When I think about the street-crossing incident now, I am startled by how much anger this small interaction stirred within me—and how difficult it was for me to move past. Looking back, it's clear that my anger had less to do with the driver's behavior and a lot more to do with my physical and mental state at the time. I was mentally and physically exhausted, unable to care for myself in all the ways I needed.

When you're unable to give yourself love and compassion, it's impossible to give it to others. Because you aren't getting what you need, holding on to anger, resentment, and unfair expectations feels good—and if you aren't careful, holding on to what you don't need becomes a regular habit.

I hope these pages will help you clarify who you are, what you want, and what you need from yourself and others. I hope they will guide you in forming boundaries, healthy expectations, and moving past people and practices that no longer serve you. Above all, I hope it will help you remain brave and open-hearted; though all things eventually come to an end, many more begin to bloom each day.

THE HEART IS
LIKE A GARDEN:
IT CAN GROW
COMPASSION OR
FEAR, RESENTMENT
OR LOVE.
WHAT SEEDS WILL
YOU PLANT THERE?

JACK KORNFIELD

Fill this garden with the seeds you'd like to plant.

In three words
I can sum up
everything I've
learned about
life:

IT
GOES
ON.

ROBERT FROST

Write a letter to yourself about a difficult experience in your life, and how proud you are for making it to the other side.

Dear Self...

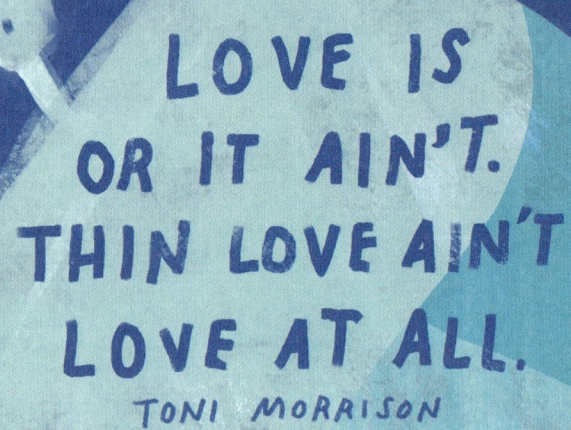

LOVE IS
OR IT AIN'T.
THIN LOVE AIN'T
LOVE AT ALL.
TONI MORRISON

Relationships where I feel
anxious, confused, or frightened:

Relationships where I feel confident,
secure, more like myself:

Cross out the relationships you'd like to let go
of. Circle the ones you'd like to strengthen.

LET GO
of believing
you shouldn't
FEEL
DEEPLY.

Fill this page in hourly, noting which feeling your body is holding on to in that moment. Breathe in, focusing on the feeling. Breathe out, letting it go.

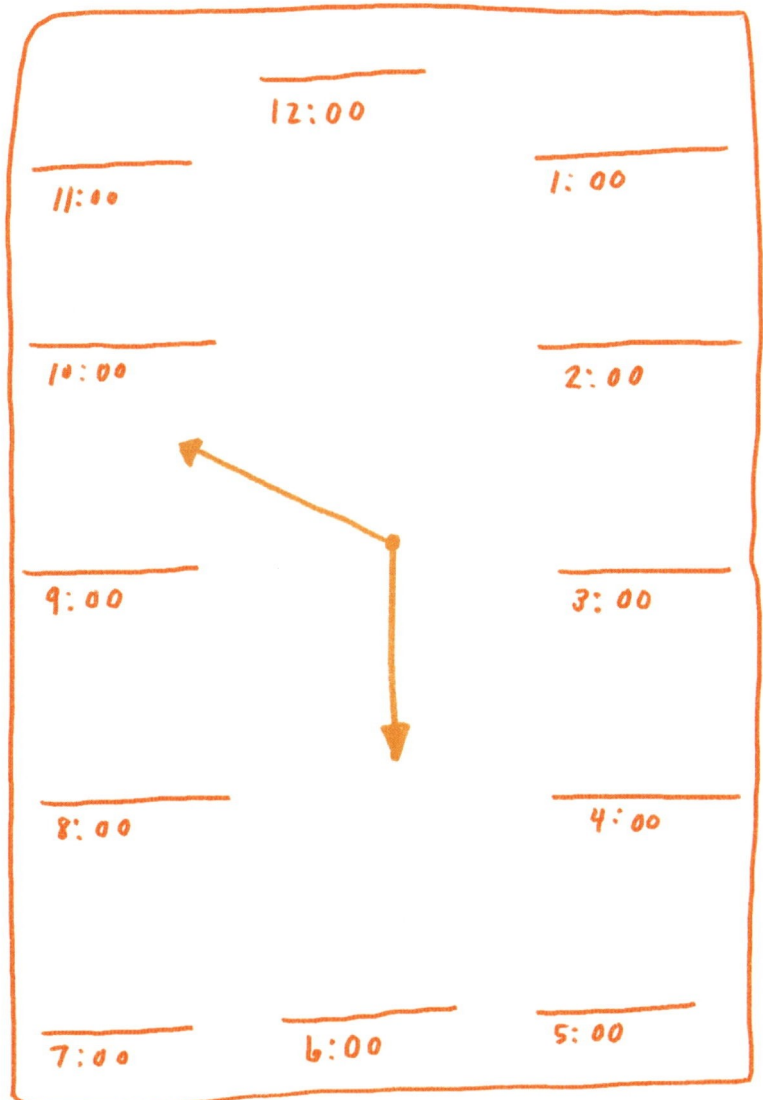

12:00

11:00

1:00

10:00

2:00

9:00

3:00

8:00

4:00

7:00

6:00

5:00

IT'S
IN VAIN
TO RECALL
THE PAST,
UNLESS IT
WORKS SOME
INFLUENCE
ON THE PRESENT.

CHARLES DICKENS

Past incident I'm dwelling on:

How it affects my present:

How it affects my future:

I'M CHOOSING
HAPPINESS
OVER SUFFERING,
I KNOW I AM. I'M MAKING
SPACE FOR THE UNKNOWN
FUTURE TO FILL UP
MY LIFE WITH YET-TO-COME
SURPRISES.

ELIZABETH GILBERT

Consider the aspects of your life that
have surprised you.

A relationship I feel grateful for:

An obstacle I never thought I'd move past:

A beautiful memory I made:

A place I never thought I'd see:

THERE ARE
YEARS THAT
ASK QUESTIONS and
YEARS THAT ANSWER.

ZORA NEALE HURSTON

List all the questions you
currently wish you had answers for.

1. _____

2. _____

3. _____

4. _____

5. _____

6. _____

7. _____

8. _____

9. _____

10. _____

Know that you will have them in time.

I GO TO NATURE
TO BE SOOTHED AND HEALED,
AND TO HAVE MY SENSES PUT IN ORDER.
JOHN BURROUGHS

Sit outside for twenty minutes without any distractions or devices. Notice how your senses heighten when you are fully present with yourself.

A soothing sight:

A smell I noticed:

A sound I heard:

A feeling I felt:

A taste in my mouth:

You have BRAINS
in your head.
YOU HAVE FEET IN
YOUR SHOES. you can
steer yourself
any direction
you choose.

YOU'RE ON
YOUR OWN.

AND YOU
KNOW WHAT
YOU KNOW.

And YOU
are the one
who'll decide
where to go.

DR. SEUSS

What do I avoid out of fear or worry?

A person:

A place:

A situation:

An experience:

What would I do if I could let go of this fear or anxiety?

A person I'd reach out to:

A place I'd visit:

A situation I'd place myself in:

An experience I'd pursue:

ISN'T IT NICE
TO THINK THAT
TOMORROW IS A
NEW DAY WITH
NO MISTAKES
IN IT YET?

L.M. MONTGOMERY

Set a timer for five minutes.

Think about what your perfect day looks like
ten years from now, and describe it here:

THE
WORLD
IS A MIRROR
IMAGE OF YOUR
MIND.
BYRON KATIE

Fill this brain with the thoughts you have most often. In its reflection, draw how each thought makes you feel.

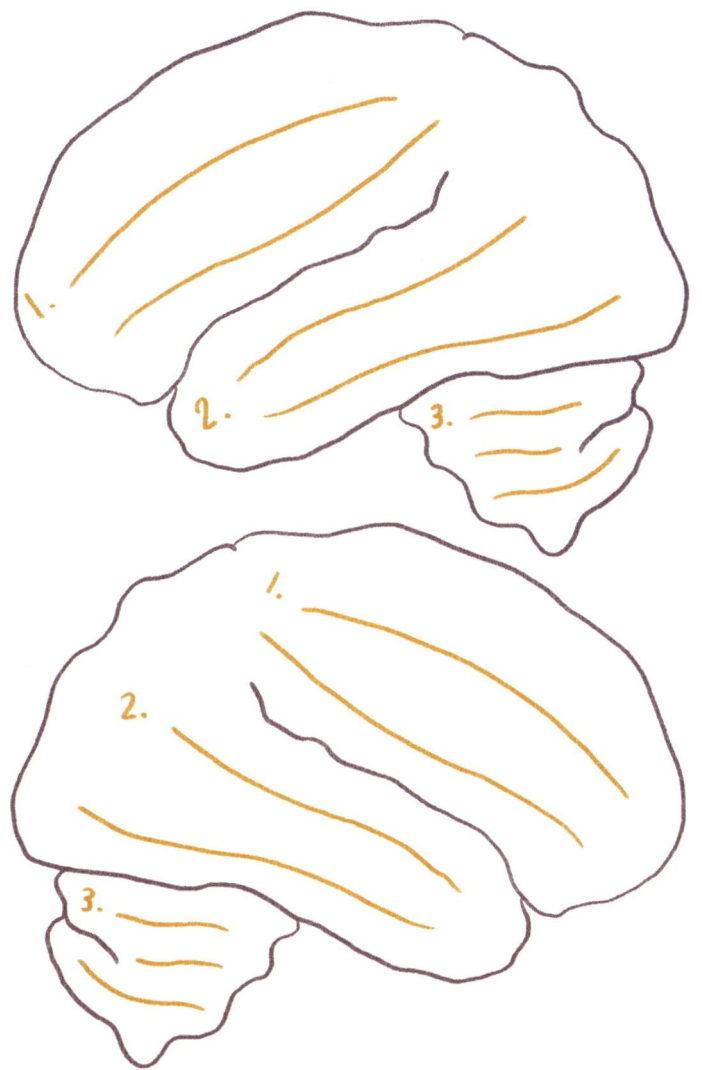

THE CURIOUS
PARADOX IS
THAT WHEN I
ACCEPT MYSELF
JUST AS I AM,
THEN I CAN
CHANGE.

CARL R. ROGERS

List 3 things you wish were different about yourself, and give yourself the patience, love, and compassion necessary to accept each one.

Then, list one action you can take to change each one over time.

An aspect of myself I'd like to change:

Why I'd like to change it:

How I can change it:

An aspect of myself I'd like to change:

Why I'd like to change it:

How I can change it:

An aspect of myself I'd like to change:

Why I'd like to change it:

How I can change it:

LIFE CHANGES IN THE INSTANT. THE ORDINARY INSTANT.

JOAN DIDION

What would I do if I didn't care what
anyone else thought?

Which do I value more, my own opinion
of myself or someone else's?

THE GREATER PART OF HUMAN ACTIVITY IS
DESIGNED TO MAKE PERMANENT THOSE EXPERIENCES
AND JOYS WHICH ARE ONLY LOVABLE BECAUSE THEY
ARE CHANGING.

ALAN WATTS

List three things that currently bring you joy, and
what you had to let go of to experience each one:

Current joy:

What I let go of to cultivate it:

Current joy:

What I let go of to cultivate it:

Current joy:

What I let go of to cultivate it:

The same
SUBSTANCE
composes us — the
tree overhead, the
stone beneath us,
the bird, the beast,
the star — WE ARE
ALL ONE, all moving
to the same end.

P.L. TRAVERS

List five things you have in common with
someone you don't get along with well.

1. _____

_____

2. _____

_____

3. _____

_____

4. _____

_____

5. _____

_____

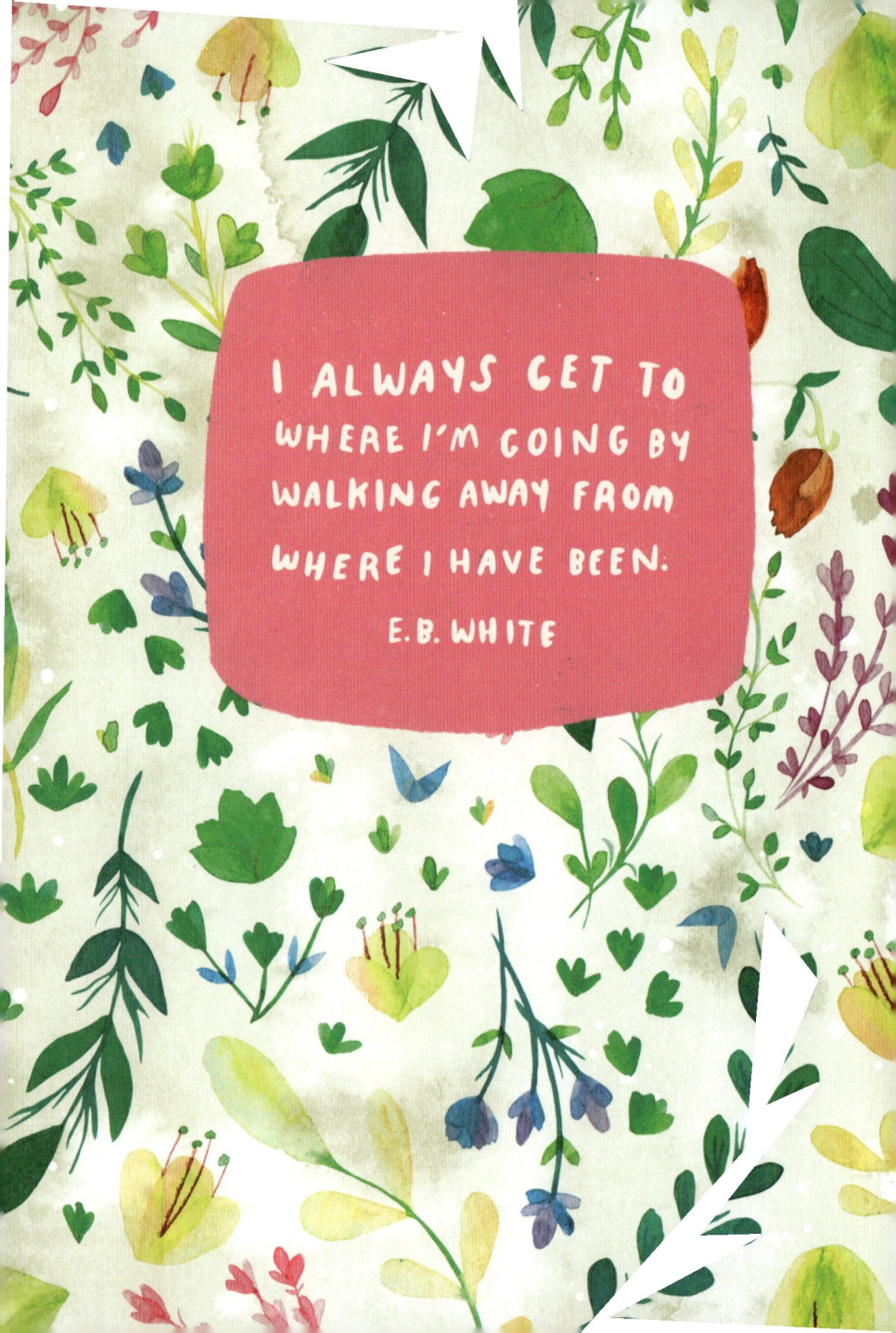

I ALWAYS GET TO WHERE I'M GOING BY WALKING AWAY FROM WHERE I HAVE BEEN.

E.B. WHITE

Something holding me back from my dream:

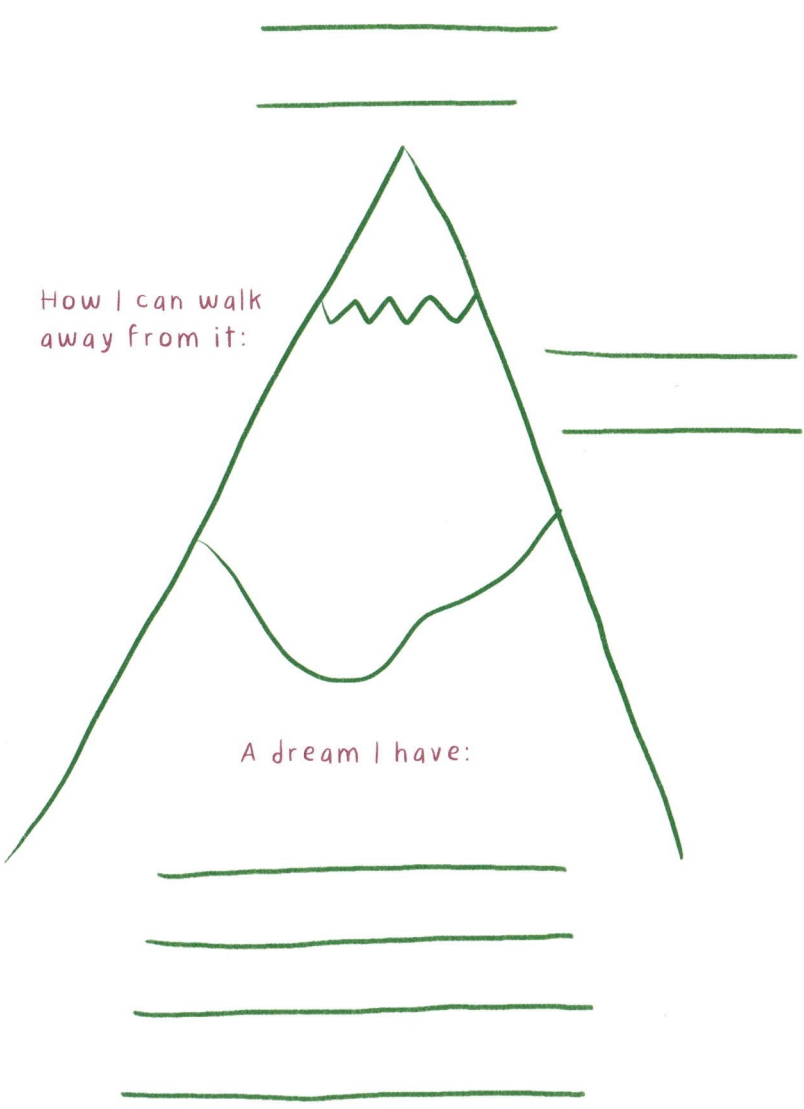

How I can walk
away from it:

A dream I have:

LET GO
of ignoring the
uncomfortable.

Feeling and grieving our emotions is a
necessary step in moving past challenging
interactions and incidents.

Practice approaching discomfort
as an observer, rather than an inhabitant.

When you feel discomfort,
notice the way it affects your body—
where do you feel tension?

How do the muscles in your face and body react?

Has your breathing changed?

Has your heartbeat quickened?

Allow your body to process the discomfort
naturally. When it's ready to do so,
allow your body to calm and relax.

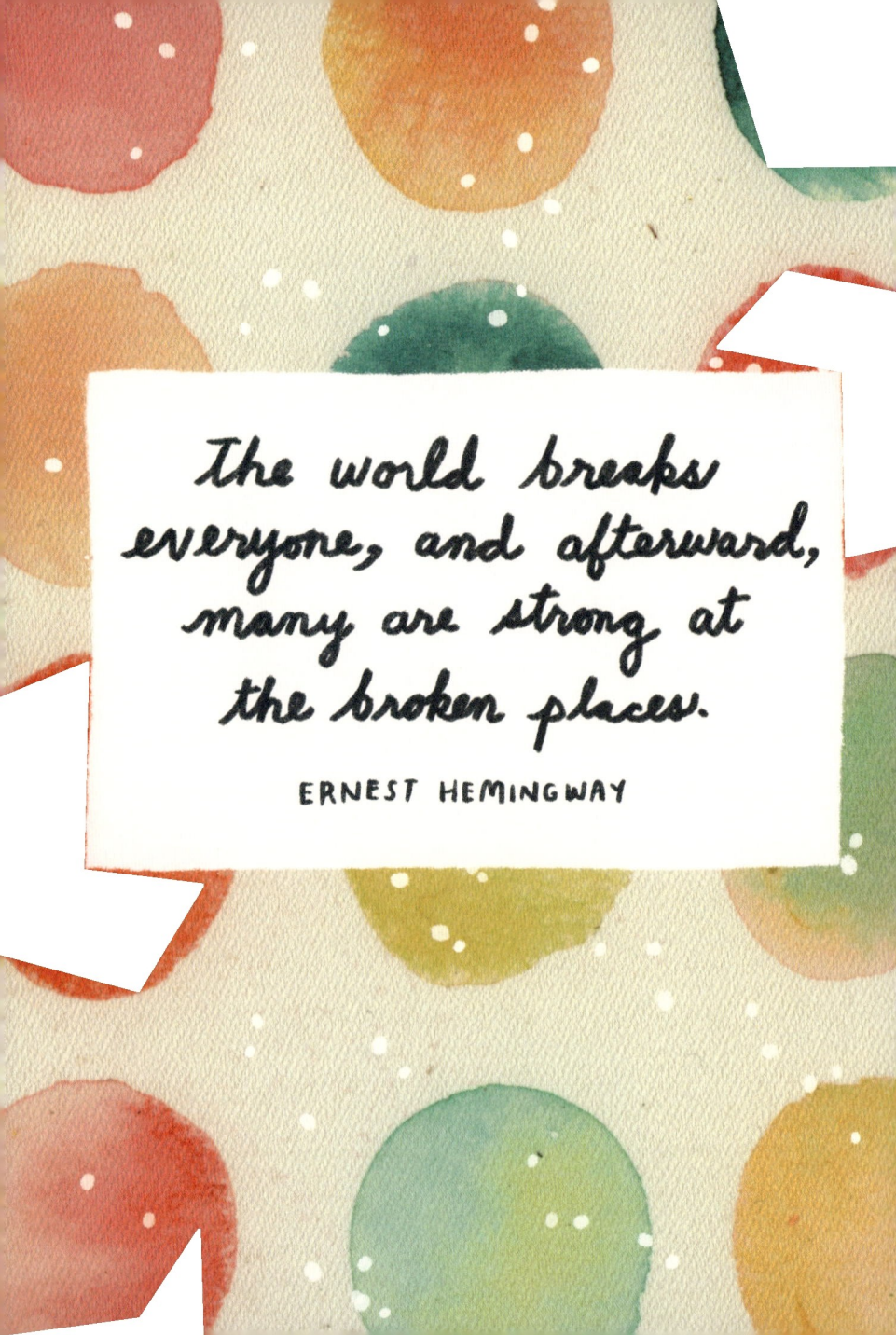

The world breaks
everyone, and afterward,
many are strong at
the broken places.

ERNEST HEMINGWAY

A broken place inside me:

The strength that stems from this place:

A broken place inside me:

The strength that stems from this place:

A broken place inside me:

The strength that stems from this place:

WE ARE MORE BLIND TO WHAT WE HAVE THAN TO WHAT WE HAVE NOT.

AUDRE LORDE

Five things I took for granted today:

1. _____
   _____
   _____

2. _____
   _____
   _____

3. _____
   _____
   _____

4. _____
   _____
   _____

5. _____
   _____
   _____

LOVE IS THE LONGING
FOR THE HALF OF OURSELVES
WE HAVE LOST.

Milan Kundera

I am most myself when...

I practice:

I speak with:

I act with:

I make time for:

I surround myself with:

I see myself as:

PATIENCE
IS THE ROAD
TO WISDOM.

KAO KALIA YANG

I practice patience with myself by:

I can practice patience with

_____ by:

(choose a person here)

THIS VERY MOMENT IS THE PERFECT
TEACHER, AND, LUCKY FOR US, IT'S
WITH US WHEREVER WE ARE.

PEMA CHODRON

In this moment,

I am learning:

I am letting go of:

I am accepting:

I am feeling:

I am.

SORROW
eats time.

BE PATIENT.

TIME
eats sorrow.

LOUISE ERDRICH

What's something painful you've found
peace with over time?

_____

_____

_____

_____

_____

_____

_____

_____

_____

_____

_____

_____

_____

ALL WE CAN KNOW
IS THAT WE KNOW
NOTHING.

AND THAT'S
THE HEIGHT OF
HUMAN WISDOM.

LEO
TOLSTOY

A person I recently disagreed with:

A possible reason for their behavior:

Does their behavior have anything to do with me?

LET GO
TO CREATE

SPACE

IN THE
PLACE
WHERE
HURT
LIVES.

Think about an experience that continues to give you grief, focusing on the way your body and mind feels when you revisit it.

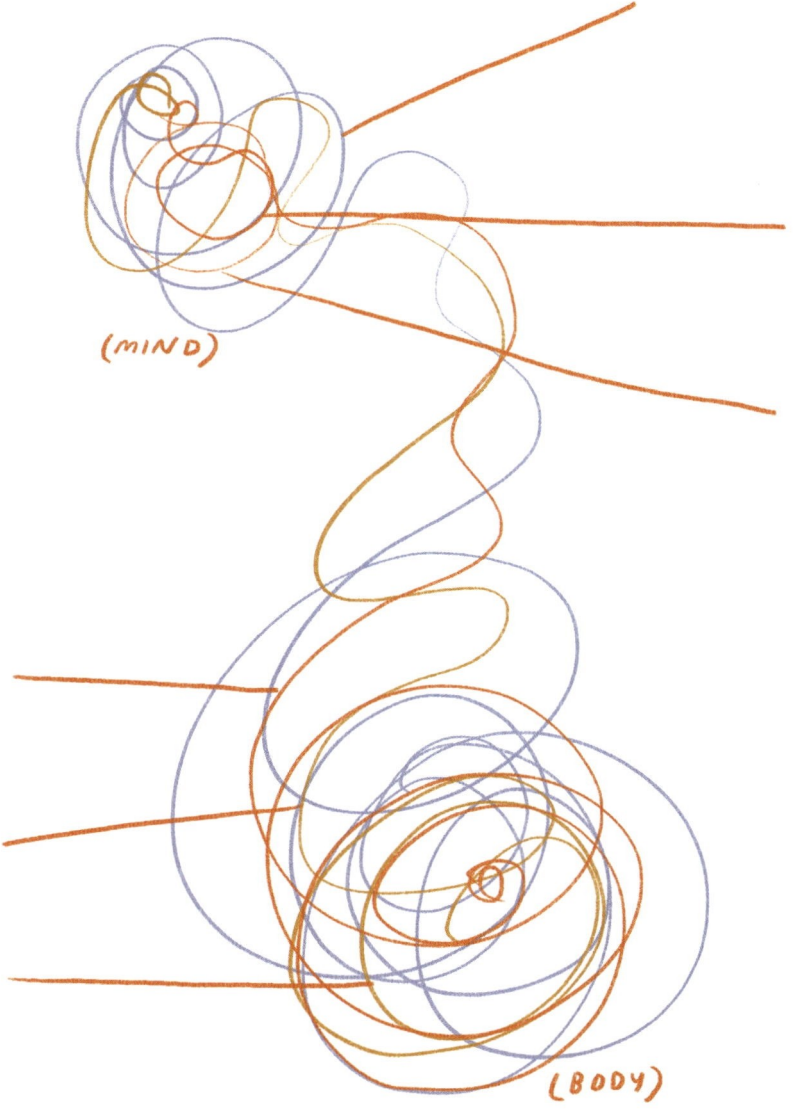

(MIND)

(BODY)

But there's
a whole world waiting,
still, and there are
good things
in it.

LOIS
LOWRY

Am I carrying any resentment toward
a person or situation?

Yes   /   No

Where in my body do I feel it?

What is it keeping me from?

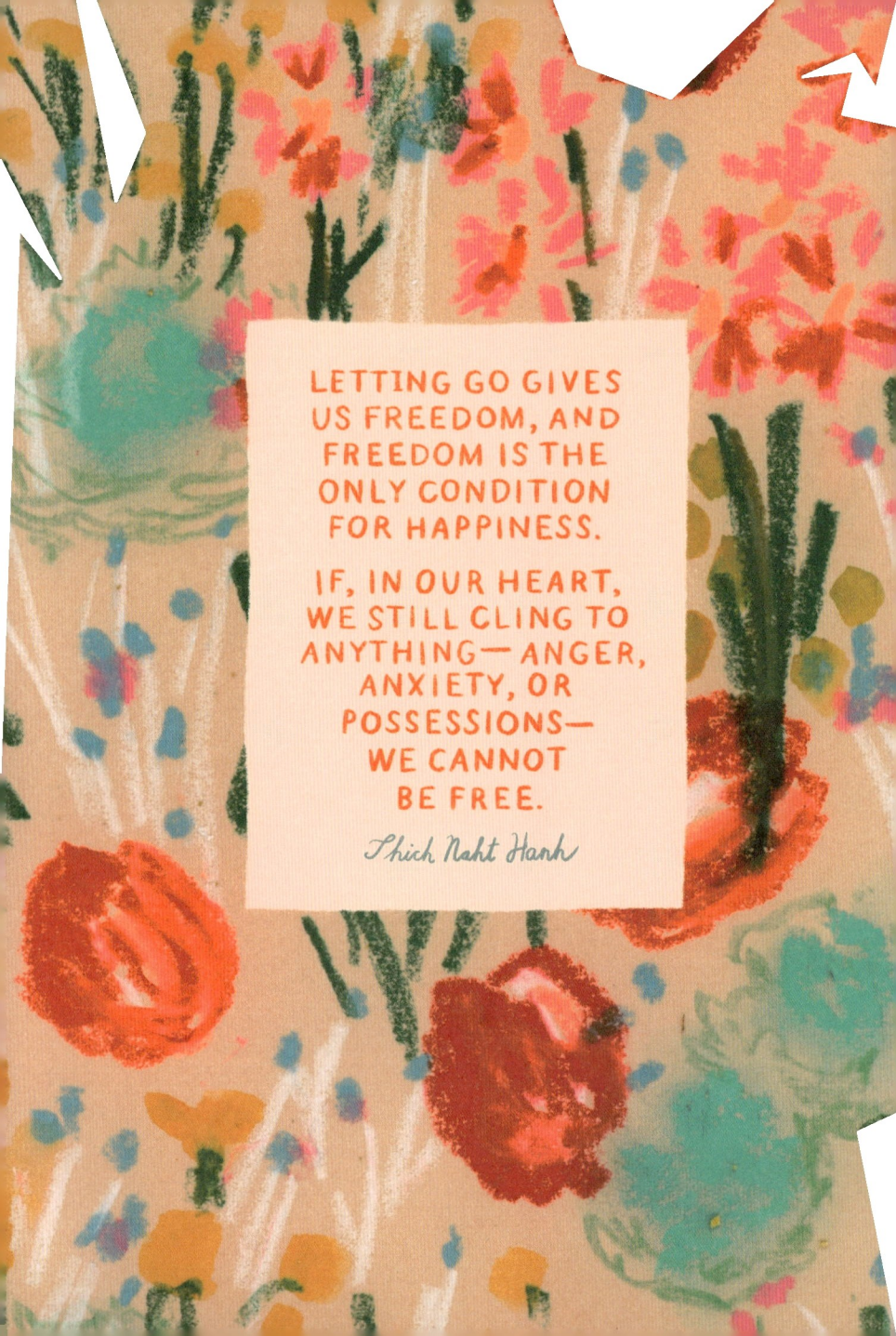

LETTING GO GIVES
US FREEDOM, AND
FREEDOM IS THE
ONLY CONDITION
FOR HAPPINESS.

IF, IN OUR HEART,
WE STILL CLING TO
ANYTHING— ANGER,
ANXIETY, OR
POSSESSIONS—
WE CANNOT
BE FREE.

Thich Naht Hanh

Fill this backpack by drawing the things
(feelings, relationships, material possessions,
ideas, beliefs) that weigh you down.

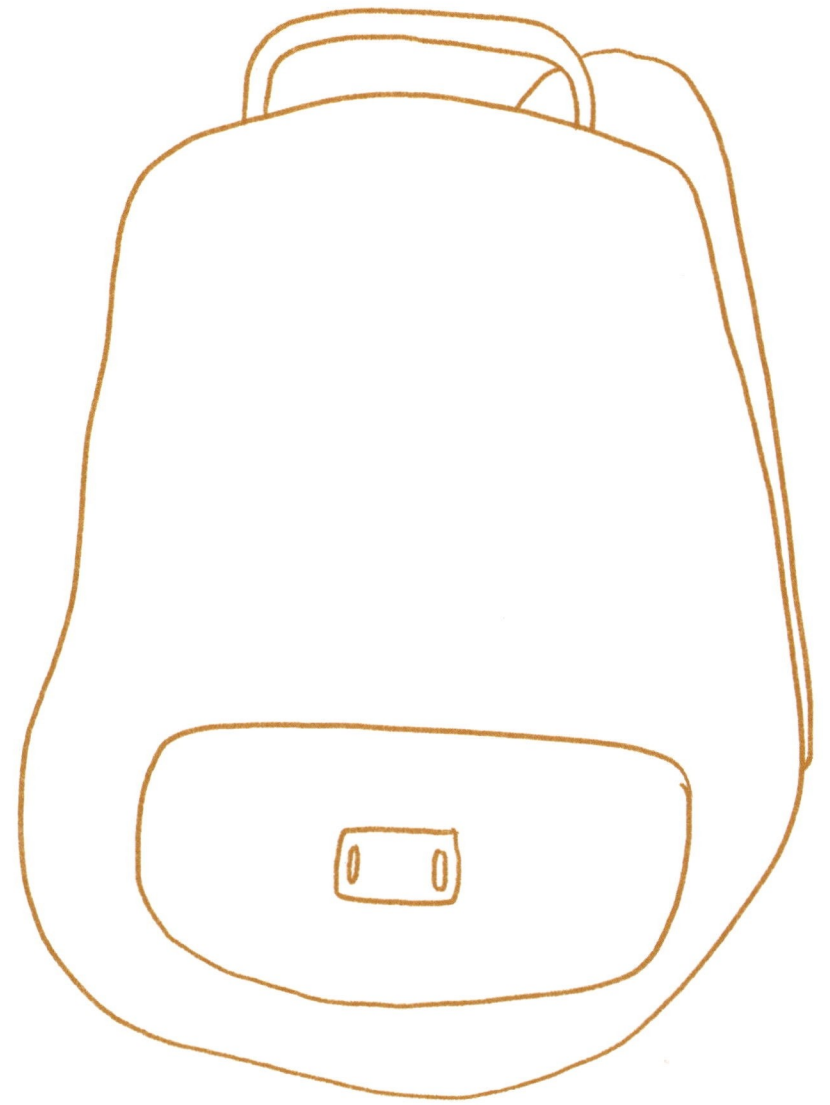

Nourish what makes
YOU FEEL CONFIDENT, CONNECTED,
CONTENTED. OPPORTUNITY WILL
rise to meet you.

OPRAH WINFREY

What makes me feel most alive?

These people:

These places:

These activities:

These habits:

These foods:

THERE IS ALWAYS
SOMETHING LEFT
TO LOVE.

Gabriel
Garcia Márquez

Think about a friendship that didn't last.

Describe two positive lessons, experiences, or moments of growth you gained from this friendship:

1. _____

_____

_____

_____

_____

_____

2. _____

_____

_____

_____

_____

ART CONSISTS OF THE PERSISTENCE OF MEMORY.

STEPHEN KING

A memory that brings you joy. Draw it here:

A memory that you avoid. Write a haiku about
it here:

A memory that gives you peace. Mark its color
and shape here:

I NEED SOLITUDE. I NEED SPACE. I NEED AIR.

Virginia Woolf

When do you feel the most free?

EVERY NEW BEGINNING COMES FROM SOME OTHER BEGINNING'S END. SENECA

Write about a new beginning that came
from an experience that ended.

The weak can never forgive. Forgiveness is the attribute of the strong.

MAHATMA GANDHI

Write a note of forgiveness to
someone who has hurt you.

Dear _____,

IF YOU CAN'T FLY
THEN RUN,
IF YOU CAN'T RUN
THEN WALK,
IF YOU CAN'T WALK,
THEN CRAWL,
BUT WHATEVER
YOU DO YOU HAVE
TO KEEP MOVING
FORWARD.

MARTIN LUTHER KING JR.

Experience I can't let go of:

The feelings that arise when I think
about this experience:

The people associated with this experience:

What I wish would happen:

A step toward forgiveness is:

TIME
MOVES
SLOWLY,
BUT
PASSES
QUICKLY.

ALICE WALKER

Three things I needed most as a child:	How I can give these to myself now:
1.	1.
2.	2.
3.	3.

Let go
OF
NEEDING
resolution
TO MOVE FORWARD.

Write about a dynamic that confuses you:

You may never understand why things are this
way—all you can do is accept how they are.

Write about how this makes you feel:

THERE IS
NO GREATER
AGONY THAN
BEARING AN
UNTOLD STORY
INSIDE YOU.

MAYA ANGELOU

Create a safe home for yourself to be vulnerable in these pages. Write about something you've never shared with anyone, without judgment or shame.

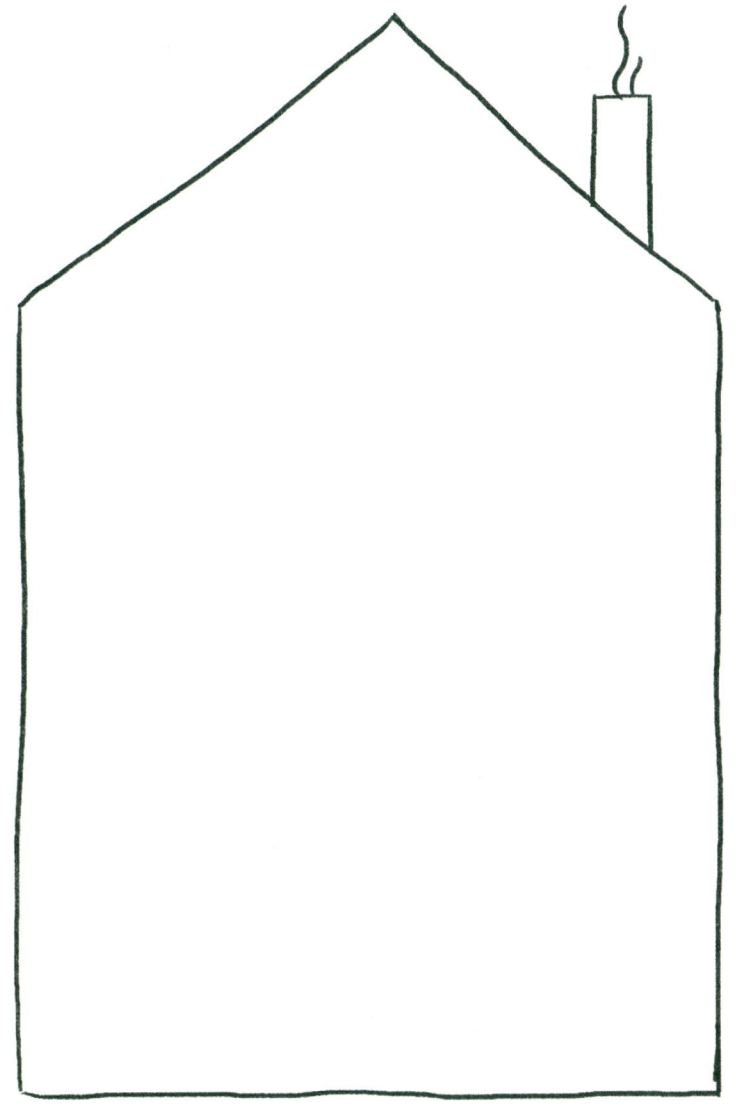

Life appears to me too short to be spent in nursing animosity or registering wrongs.

CHARLOTTE BRONTË

Blaming others keeps us in resentment and anger, preventing us from accepting our own responsibility or moving toward growth. Think of a situation where you were wronged by another person.

What could you have done differently to decrease animosity and increase understanding?

What can you do now to repair and heal?

If you could have an honest conversation with this person, what would you say?

THERE WAS
ANOTHER LIFE THAT
I MIGHT HAVE HAD,
BUT I AM HAVING
THIS ONE.

KAZUO
ISHIGURO

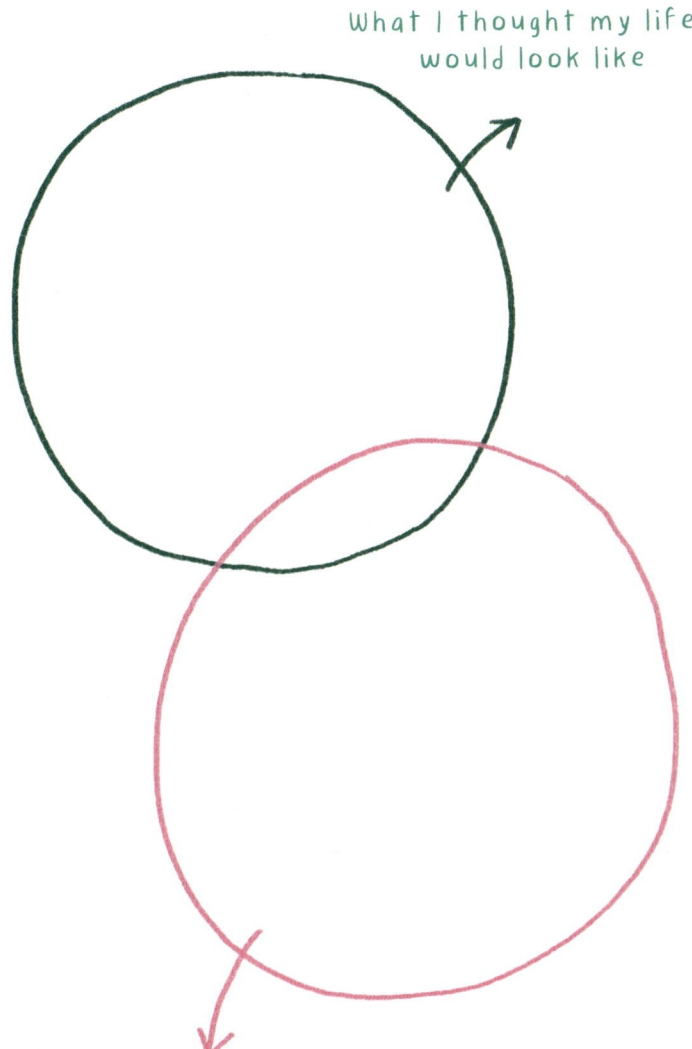

What I thought my life
would look like

What my life looks like

Some changes look negative on the surface,
but you will soon realize that space is
**BEING CREATED IN YOUR LIFE FOR
SOMETHING NEW TO EMERGE.** Eckhart Tolle

List three challenging events that took place over the last few years:

*

*

*

One lesson you learned from each experience:

*

*

*

One surprising outcome that arose from each experience:

*

*

*

FINDING BEAUTY IN A BROKEN WORLD IS CREATING BEAUTY IN THE WORLD WE FIND. TERRY TEMPEST WILLIAMS

A global or political issue that overwhelms me:

An action I can take to make the world better:

WHERE
YOU TEND
A ROSE,
MY LAD,
A THISTLE
CANNOT
GROW.

FRANCES
HODGSON
BURNETT

Circle the values you want to live by:

BOLDNESS	ACCOUNTABILITY	ACHIEVEMENT
WEALTH	COMMUNITY	COMMITMENT
THOUGHTFUL	GRATITUDE	AMBITION
RESPECTFUL	ADVENTURE	BALANCE
EQUALITY	COMPASSION	FREEDOM
SELFLESS	ALTRUISM	PLEASURE
COMMUNITY	SELF-GROWTH	FRIENDSHIP
OPENNESS	HONESTY	KINDNESS
CURIOSITY	TRUST	CONFIDENCE
ENCOURAGEMENT	CREATIVITY	SECURITY
RESILIENCE	LEADERSHIP	HEALTH
FAIRNESS	INDEPENDENCE	PEACE
DIGNITY	SUCCESS	OPTIMISM
CHALLENGE	TRUST	PATIENCE
WISDOM	DISCIPLINE	LEARNING

WE ARE WHAT WE PRETEND TO BE, SO WE MUST BE CAREFUL ABOUT WHAT WE PRETEND TO BE. KURT VONNEGUT

Identify three behaviors or actions
that don't align with your values.

1. _____

_____

_____

2. _____

_____

_____

3. _____

_____

_____

Let go of quieting yourself to
make others more comfortable.

List three incidents where behaving according to
your values upset someone else.

1. _____

_____

_____

_____

2. _____

_____

_____

_____

3. _____

_____

_____

_____

BOUNDARIES ARE THE DISTANCE AT WHICH I
CAN LOVE YOU AND ME SIMULTANEOUSLY.

Prentis Hemphill

Person or
situation:

How my values are
being disrespected:

Boundary I can set:

Identify habits you've formed that you want to let go of. Replace each one with a habit you'd like to form instead.

OLD HABIT	NEW HABIT

YOU CAN'T
GO BACK AND
CHANGE THE
BEGINNING,
BUT YOU CAN
START WHERE
YOU ARE AND
CHANGE THE
ENDING.

UNKNOWN

Consider a situation you wish were
turning out differently.

What action can you take
now to rectify it?

Who controls the past controls the future. WHO CONTROLS THE PRESENT CONTROLS THE PAST.

GEORGE ORWELL

The only person you can truly change is yourself.

How do you want to make others feel?

How do you want to make yourself feel?

We have to
belong to ourselves as
much as we need to belong
to others. BRENÉ BROWN

What is something you wish others
would accept about you?

Do you accept it about yourself?

IF YOU WANT TO BECOME WHOLE, LET YOURSELF BE PARTIAL.
IF YOU WANT TO BECOME STRAIGHT, LET YOURSELF BE CROOKED.
IF YOU WANT TO BECOME FULL, LET YOURSELF BE EMPTY.
IF YOU WANT TO BE REBORN, LET YOURSELF DIE.
IF YOU WANT TO BE GIVEN EVERYTHING, GIVE EVERYTHING UP.

LAO TZU

To let go of perfection, I can stop:

I am a fallible human. A mistake I must accept:

An expectation I will let go of:

WHEN WE
REJOICE IN
OUR FULLNESS, THEN
WE CAN PART WITH
OUR FRUITS WITH
JOY. RABINDRANATH
TAGORE

List ten attributes you love about yourself:

1. _____

2. _____

3. _____

4. _____

5. _____

6. _____

7. _____

8. _____

9. _____

10. _____

Remember that no one can take these from you.

LET THE RAIN KISS YOU.

LET THE RAIN BEAT UPON
YOUR HEAD WITH SILVER
LIQUID DROPS.

LET THE RAIN SING
YOU A LULLABY.

LANGSTON
HUGHES

Identify a transformative moment in your life

What joy did it bring you?

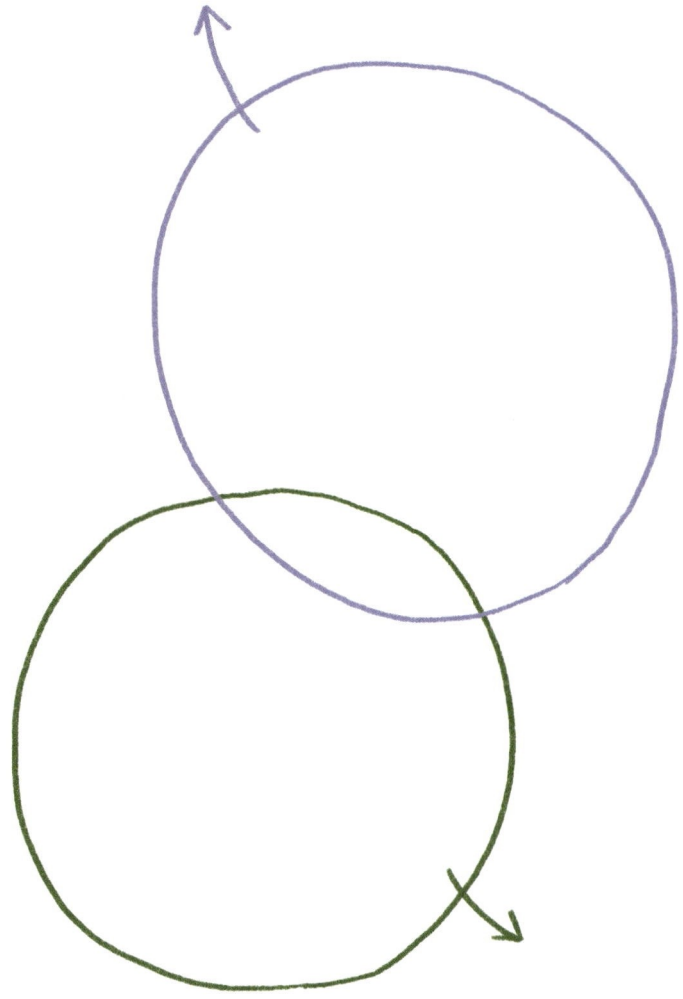

What sorrow did it bring you?

Life is to be lived, not controlled; AND HUMANITY IS WON BY CONTINUING TO PLAY IN FACE OF CERTAIN DEFEAT.

Ralph Ellison

WHO DO I WANT TO BE?

Three words you believe others would use to describe you:

1. _____

2. _____

3. _____

Three words you want to be described as:

1. _____

2. _____

3. _____

An action to bring you from A to B:

1. _____

2. _____

3. _____

Time is the
longest distance
between two places.

TENNESSEE WILLIAMS

What did I most want for myself as a child?

What do I most want for myself now?

Wintering...
*is the courage
to stare down the
worst parts of
our experience
and to commit to
healing them the
best we can.*

KATHERINE MAY

Write a letter to the parts of yourself that feel the most alone, hurt, and vulnerable. Express your understanding and compassion, and outline what you most wish for this part of yourself—whether that's healing, forgiveness, or to simply feel seen.

Dear Self,

Once you are Real
you can't be ugly,
except to people who
don't understand.
MARGERY WILLIAMS

Think of a person you can truly be yourself around.

Write about that person
and how they make you feel.

HOPE IS THE THING WITH FEATHERS—
THAT PERCHES IN THE SOUL—
AND SINGS THE TUNE WITHOUT WORDS
AND NEVER STOPS— AT ALL—.

EMILY DICKINSON

If I knew it would work out the way I'd like it to...

I'd stop:

*

*

*

*

*

I'd begin:

*

*

*

*

*

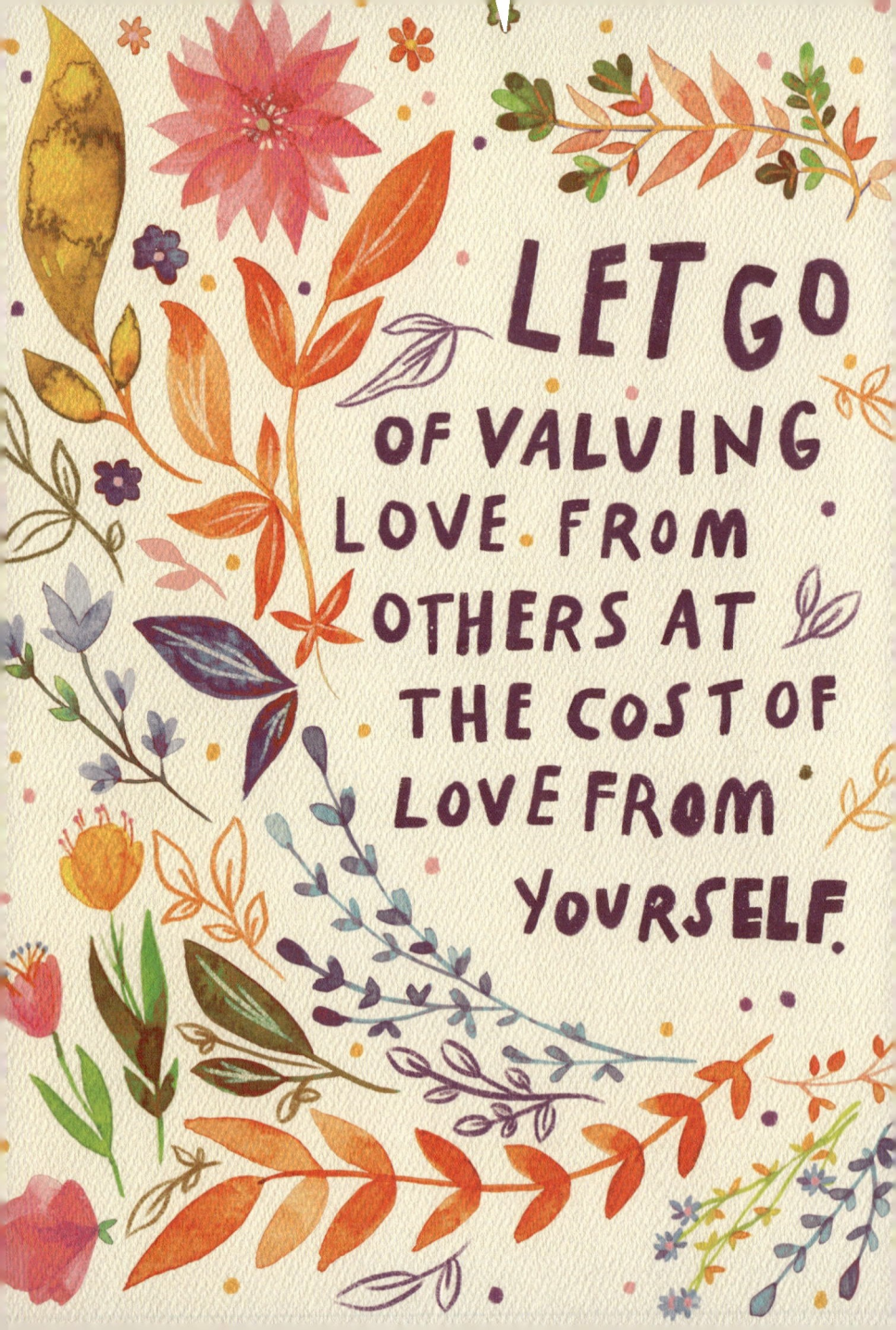

LET GO OF VALUING LOVE FROM OTHERS AT THE COST OF LOVE FROM YOURSELF.

Write down the words you've always wanted to hear from someone else—words of validation, self-worth, and acceptance. Stand in front of a mirror and read them aloud to yourself.

THE
ONLY
WAY

OUT OF THE

LABYRINTH

OF SUFFERING IS TO
FORGIVE.

JOHN GREEN

I forgive myself for:

I forgive myself for:

I forgive myself for:

I forgive myself for:

I forgive myself for:

Bibliography

Angelou, Maya. *I Know Why the Caged Bird Sings*. Bantam Books, 1993.

Bianco, Margery Williams. *The Velveteen Rabbit*. Avon, 1987.

Brontë, Charlotte. *Jane Eyre*. Penguin, 2003.

Brown, Brené. *Atlas of the Heart: Mapping Meaningful Connection and the Language of Human Experience*. Random House, 2021.

Burnett, Frances Hodgson. *Sara Crewe, or What Happened at Miss Michin's*. Echo Library, 2007.

Burroughs, John. *Time and Change*. Project Gutenberg, 2004.

Chödrön, Pema. *When Things Fall Apart: Heart Advice for Difficult Times*. Shambhala, 2000.

Dickens, Charles. *David Copperfield*. Penguin Classics, 2004.

Didion, Joan. *The Year of Magical Thinking*. Vintage, 2007.

Ellison, Ralph. *Invisible Man*. Vintage, 1995.

Erdrich, Louise. *LaRose*. Harper, 2016.

Frost, Robert. "Robert Frost's Secret." Interview by Ray Josephs. "This Week Magazine" in *The Cincinnati Enquirer*, quote page 2, column 1, 1954.

Gandhi, Mahatma. *All Men Are Brothers: Autobiographical Reflections*. Bloomsbury Academic, 2005.

Gilbert, Elizabeth. *Eat, Pray, Love: One Woman's Search for Everything Across Italy, India and Indonesia*. Riverhead Books, 2007.

Green, John. *Looking for Alaska*. Speak, 2006.

Hanh, Thich Nhat. *The Heart of the Buddha's Teaching: Transforming Suffering into Peace, Joy, and Liberation*. Broadway Books, 1999.

Hemingway, Ernest. *A Farewell to Arms*. Arrow Books, 2004.

Hemphill, Prentis. *What It Takes to Heal: How Transforming Ourselves Can Change the World*. Random House, 2024.

Hughes, Langston. "An April Rain Song," *The Brownies' Book*. April 1921.

Hurston, Zora Neale. *Their Eyes Were Watching God*. Amistad, 2006.

Ishiguro, Kazuo. Conversation with Lewis Burke Frumkes, *The Writer*, volume 114, number 5, May 2001, collected in *Conversations with Kazuo Ishiguro*, p. 189.

Katie, Byron. *A Friendly Universe: Sayings to Inspire and Challenge You*. TarcherPerigee, 2013.

King Jr., Martin Luther, "Keep Moving from This Mountain." Spelman College, 10 April, 1960. Atlanta, Georgia.

King, Stephen. *Misery*. New English Library, 1988.

Kornfield, Jack. *Buddha's Little Instruction Book*. Bantam Books, 1994.

Kundera, Milan. *The Unbearable Lightness of Being.* Harper Perennial, 2009.

Lorde, Audre. *Sister Outsider: Essays and Speeches.* Crossing Press, 1984.

Lowry, Lois. *A Summer to Die.* Laurel Leaf, 1983.

Márquez, Gabriel García. *One Hundred Years of Solitude.* Avon Books, 1970.

May, Katherine. *Wintering: The Power of Rest and Retreat in Difficult Times.* Riverhead Books, 2020.

Montgomery, L. M. *Anne of Green Gables.* Signet, 2003.

Morrison, Toni. *Beloved.* Vintage Books, 2007.

Orwell, George. *1984.* Secker & Warburg, 1949.

Rogers, Carl R. *On Becoming a Person: A Therapist's View of Psychotherapy.* Mariner Books, 1995.

Seuss, Dr. *Oh, the Places You'll Go.* Random House Books for Young Readers, 1990.

Tagore, Rabindranath. *Gitanjali.* Rupa Publications Private Limited, 2002.

Tolle, Eckhart. *The Power of Now: A Guide to Spiritual Enlightenment.* New World Library, 2004.

Tolstoy, Leo. *War and Peace.* Oxford University Press, 1998.

Travers, P.L. *Mary Poppins.* Clarion Books, 2006.

Tzu, Lao. *Tao Te Ching.* Vintage, 1989.

Vonnegut, Kurt. *Mother Night.* Dial Press, 1999.

Walker, Alice. *The Color Purple.* Penguin Books, 2019.

Watts, Alan W. *The Wisdom of Insecurity*. Vintage Books, 1951.

Williams, Tennessee. *The Glass Menagerie*. Turtleback Books, 1999.

Williams, Terry Tempest. *Finding Beauty in a Broken World*.
Pantheon, 2008.

Winfrey, Oprah. *The Path Made Clear: Discovering Your Life's
Direction and Purpose*. Flatiron Books, 2019.

Woolf, Virginia. *A Writer's Diary*. Mariner Books Classics, 2003.

Yang, Kao Kalia. *The Latehomecomer: A Hmong Family Memoir*.
Coffee House Press, 2008.

Acknowledgments

With love and gratitude for my children and husband, who encourage me to leave the past where it belongs—and who help me build a greater beauty in every tomorrow.

With many thanks to Marian, my editor, and Laurie, my agent, for guiding my ideas into the world with continued encouragement and support. I am ever so grateful.

About the Author

Meera Lee Patel is the self-taught artist and best-selling author of several books on mental and emotional health, including *Start Where You Are: A Journal for Self-Exploration and How it Feels to Find Yourself: Navigating Life's Changes with Purpose, Clarity, and Heart.* Her books and journals have sold over a million copies worldwide and are translated into more than a dozen languages.

She lives with her family in St. Louis, Missouri. For more about Meera and her work, please visit www.meeralee.com or find her online @meeraleepatel.

ALSO BY
Meera Lee Patel

BOOKS

 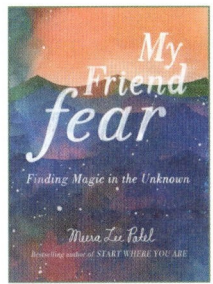

JOURNALS

 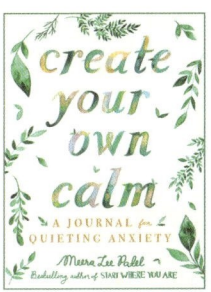

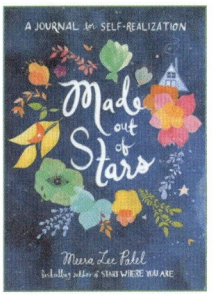 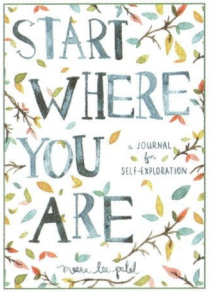

MEERALEE.COM